# The Blanket

AN ILLUSTRATED HISTORY OF THE

## HUDSON'S BAY POINT BLANKET

Harold Tichenor

A QUANTUM BOOK
Produced for
HUDSON'S BAY COMPANY

# CONTENTS

York Factory, on the shores of the Hayes River, was the headquarters of the Company. Furs, point blankets, and other trade goods once filled its vast holds.

# PROLOGUE

For well over two centuries, the Hudson's Bay point blanket
has been a Canadian icon associated with legends of exploration and the
development of the nation. Hudson's Bay Company (Hbc) point blankets
are the standard by which all other wool blankets are measured. Since
1780, Hudson's Bay Company has commissioned and marketed these fine
English-made woollen products. But, while hundreds of thousands of
these point blankets have been purchased over the decades, many owners
are unaware of the fascinating traditions and history surrounding them.
The story is a long and fascinating one — one that offers a unique
window into the history of Canada and North America.

The characteristic markings of a point blanket are visible in this mid-nineteenth
century painting by Cornelius Krieghoff.

# THE BIRTH OF AN ICON

Since the middle of the seventeenth century, wool blankets, trade axes, iron- and copperware, knives, and firearms served as the principal European goods offered in trade to the peoples of the First Nations of North America. But of all these trade goods there is probably no more emblematic an item of the "Indian Fur Trade" than the Hudson's Bay point blanket. Point blankets were a material link between two cultures in transition: the product of the industrializing textile manufacturing villages in England and a practical and cultural "tool" for the peoples of a variety of North American First Nations cultures. While point blankets have always been manufactured in a range of colours and basic patterns, they are all made of wool and have one or more stripes (also called "headings," "bars," or "bands") near each end. But, most importantly, the point blanket bears a number of short threads of wool yarn most often woven or sewn into a corner of the blanket's central field. These lines are called "points" and were intended to identify the size, and thus the value, of the blanket.

Men working for the various fur trading companies ventured far from their European homes seeking to acquire the pelts of a number of North American mammals, principally those of the arctic fox, the lynx, and perhaps most importantly, the beaver. For generations the undercoat of the fur of the beaver was the prime source of the fibres used to make European gentlemen's top hats. In addition, the tanned and dressed pelts themselves were used to make fine coats, and the castoreum from the beaver's scent glands (a natural

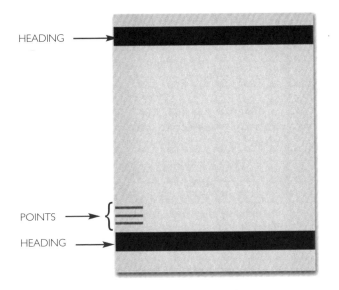

HEADING ⟶

POINTS ⟶ {
HEADING ⟶

7

## FOR WANT OF A HAT

**A** fashion for hats drew the Company to Hudson Bay. In the seventeenth century, everyone of style and note wanted a beaver hat — one made of the felt from the undercoat of the beaver's pelt. Once sheared from the pelt, this fine dense fur, consisting of thousands of short barbed hairs, could be pressed into a glossy felt that was waterproof and could be worked into many different styles (right).

Many early illustrations of beavers and their ways were done by artists who had never actually seen them. (Above) This 1777 engraving shows beavers living in apartment-style colonies.

source of acetylsalicylic acid — aspirin) was medicinally used for treating aches and pains. Canadian furs were highly valued in Europe because the cold winter climate of the Arctic and Subarctic regions makes for particularly luxuriant pelts. The constant eastward flow of these prime furs from North America to Europe has continued since the mid-seventeenth century up to the present day.

While there were a number of fur trading companies operating in the North American wilderness, most of which dealt in similar goods in trading for furs, historically the point blanket is most closely associated with Hbc. Founded in 1670 as "The Governor and Company of Adventurers of England tradeing into Hudson's Bay," Hudson's Bay Company rapidly became the aristocracy of the North American fur trade. Reflecting the economic importance of the beaver and the arduous demands of the fur trade, the

Hudson's Bay Company's coat of arms sports four beavers and the motto "Pro Pelle Cutem," which can be loosely translated as "for furs we risk our hides."

But, contrary to popular opinion, Hudson's Bay Company was not the first to introduce the point blanket into the fur trade. In fact, "points," the small lines of wool woven or threaded into one corner of a blanket's field, appear to have been used first on blankets manufactured in France during the sixteenth century. It is probable that the word "point" itself derived from the French verb *empointer,* meaning to make threaded stitches on cloth. The "pointed blanket" at that time was offered in general European trade as a household item for acquisition by middle-class residents, and later to the early settlers of North America. The number of points on a blanket was the weaver's indication of the blanket's intended finished size, and continues to be so today.

By the 1690s, the French traders in North America had introduced the "point system" in their blanket trade. For the fur trade, blankets of one to four points were most common. However, blankets with up to twelve points have been reported from this period, but most probably for the non-Aboriginal trade. It is likely that point blankets were being manufactured in England well before

## COMPANY OF ADVENTURERS

**P**rince Rupert of the Rhine (right), a cousin of King Charles II of England, persuaded some of the wealthiest and best-connected men in England to found a trading company that would operate in the wilderness of North America. At Whitehall Palace in London, on May 2, 1670, King Charles authorized the Royal Charter that created "The Governor and Company of Adventurers of England tradeing into Hudson's Bay." Thus Hudson's Bay Company, the world's oldest continuously operating trading company, was born. The Charter (above), which features a portrait of the King worked into the letter C in his name, is now kept at Hbc's head office in Toronto. (Below) The Company's initials are emblazoned on the bow of this canoe.

the American Revolution, since by the 1770s the use of point blankets was quite common among the English colonists and it is doubtful that they would have acquired them from French manufacturers due to trade restrictions between England and France. In the middle of that decade there are references indicating that four-point blankets were standard issue for the American colonial militiamen. The Museum of the Fur Trade in Chadron, Nebraska, has in its collection a point blanket carried as part of the kit of an American Revolutionary War soldier. As well, coats made from point blankets, called "Canadian blanket coats," were used by British troops serving during the American Revolution.

While it is certain that Hudson's Bay Company had woollen blankets available for trade on a regular basis from its inception in 1670, the Company did not formally adopt the point blanket as a staple of trade until about 1780. On the recommendation of Germain Maugenest, a French trader with experience in the Mississippi territories, as well as in the Canadian fur trade, the Company started to offer point blankets to compete with the already well-recognized practices of the Montreal-based fur trading companies. However, the scale of Hbc's trade in point blankets grew so rapidly that by the third decade of the nineteenth century the term "Hudson's Bay Blanket" had become synonymous with the point blanket.

(Opposite) A selection of the goods the Company offered, including pots, rifles, and the ever-popular point blanket. (Right) A Native examines a point blanket for its quality in this drawing by C.W. Jeffreys.

# "THE MOST INDISPENSABLE PIECE OF CLOTHING..."

(Below) Point blankets can be seen being used as sleeping robes in this scene from a Cree wigwam. The Cree did much of the inland travelling and trading for the Company. (Opposite) Natives at a typical Company trading post.

**W**hile these textiles were manufactured as, and called "blankets," their main use among Native North Americans was as a form of clothing. Smaller blankets suitable for wearing by children were designated with one, one and a half, or two points; women's wearing robes were two and a half to three points; and men's wearing robes were three to three and a half points. Proper sleeping robes were generally three and a half to four points or even larger. More often than not, particularly in the Canadian North, the sleeping robes were left as unseparated pairs, with the user able to slip between the folded blankets, not unlike a modern sleeping bag.

Contrary to popular belief, the number of points on a blanket was not originally intended to equal the value of the blanket in the quantity of beaver pelts for which it was traded. That equivalency was more coincidental than planned, and is the result of the peculiarities of Hbc's trading practices. During the seventeenth and eighteenth centuries in the North American "wilderness," currency in the form of coins and notes was extremely rare. The need to rationalize the comparative value of trade goods required the establishment of an alternative "money supply." Hudson's

(Right) In this painting, Hbc Inland Governor Simpson is welcomed by the Company's West Coast representative James Douglas while trappers and Natives look on. Several of the Natives are wrapped in a point blanket or dressed in a point blanket coat or "capote." (Opposite) Currency, in the form of coins and notes such as these, was so rare that the beaver pelt and later the point blanket itself became standards for trade values.

Bay Company had long established a system of economic exchange that relied on a readily recognizable commodity, the "made beaver." Just as the "buckskin" was used as a form of currency in the English colonies, the beaver skin served the function of a monetary unit in the far reaches of the Canadian North. One unit (or made beaver) equalled an adult beaver in prime condition. Often the value of the point blankets in made beaver did equal their point size. However, there were times when beaver pelts were particularly scarce so that a blanket could be had for fewer beaver skins than its point size would indicate. In the early eighteenth century, a blanket in Montreal might command five beaver skins while a similar sized one in Boston could be had for only one or two beaver skins. A May 1780 letter from the Governor and Committee of the Company to Thomas Hutchins, Chief Factor at Fort Albany on James Bay, notified him of the very first shipment of point blankets and the price to be charged for them:

| The one Pointed Blankets are to be charged at | 1 Beaver each |
|---|---|
| one and half pointed | 2 Beavers each |
| two pointed | $2^1/_2$ Beavers each |

Nevertheless, since the coincidence was quite common, it is a useful guide to the comparative value of these two items over the initial decades of the trade. For some cultures, the point blanket itself became a standard for daily trade values, a form of currency like the made beaver. By the mid-nineteenth century, the Tsimshian of the Northwest Coast of Canada used the two-point blanket to replace their earlier more variable fur-based currencies. Similarly, the Haida used the two and a half point Hbc blanket as a form of currency in the late nineteenth century.

It is well documented that First Nations customers were very demanding when it came to determining quality in trading for blankets and other trade goods. Michel Begon, the Intendant of New France, reported that it was not uncommon for Native buyers to lightly scorch a discreet corner of the blanket, burning away the nap to allow a closer inspection of the quality and tightness of the actual weave. As well, members of each Native cultural tradition had strong opinions on the shades of each colour that were acceptable. Since, for the peoples of many First Nations, the colours themselves had significant spiritual meaning, the strength of the colour was a critical factor in blanket selection. And, of course, it would be an error to dismiss the importance of "being in style," for Native Canadians and Americans were just as style conscious as people of any other contemporary cultural group.

Dr. Aurel Krause and his brother, Arthur, spent a winter among the Tlingit in 1881-2 carrying out ethnographic research for the Geographical Society of Bremen:

> *A woolen blanket now is the most indispensable piece of clothing of an Indian. It is thrown loosely over the shoulder and worn in a togalike fashion. Blankets of blue and white are preferred (among the Tlingit) but even here fashion changes, much to the chagrin of the traders.*

The point blanket was adopted with enthusiasm by most of the Aboriginal peoples of the West. While the wearing of blankets long predated the advent of European trade, the advantages of blankets made from wool, their high insulating properties in relation to their comparatively light weight and their availability in a variety of bright and attractive colours, led to their ready acceptance by the peoples of many differing cultural traditions.

A Souteaux Native and his family travel near Lake Winnipeg in winter.

## TRAPPERS AND TRADERS

Diverse groups among the Aboriginal peoples adopted the Hudson's Bay point blanket as seen in these early twentieth century photos of three members of the Blackfoot First Nations wearing Hbc blanket coats (below) and (opposite) a Haida woman wearing a point blanket.

It is often assumed that the English fur trade companies wantonly exploited the Native peoples of North America. But if the manufacturing cost of the blankets, the market value of the furs in Europe, and the early rule of thumb of one point per made beaver are all taken into account, a more balanced picture emerges. English craftsmen laboured far longer making the blankets than did Inuit or Cree trappers obtaining the blanket's equivalency in beaver pelts. And Hudson's Bay Company also incurred great expense in shipping goods both ways across the perilous North Atlantic and in penetrating some of the most remote areas of British North America.

The peoples of the First Nations enthusiastically took up trapping for trade and allowed it to augment their more traditional means of economic survival. So much so that the Nations closest to the trading posts attempted to monopolize trade with the Europeans by using their newly acquired firearms to keep the more distant, less well-armed tribes away from the posts.

To assume that the Native Canadians were merely exploited dupes of the fur traders is to greatly underestimate them. In fact, it was the traders who adopted "native ways" and not the converse. The Scots and French who came to North America often spent their whole lives working in the fur trade. More often than not, they took

(Left) Cornelius Krieghoff depicted an 1850 trader bartering with an Aboriginal family over blankets and trade goods.

Native wives and learned the local dialects and customs. The rigours of living in the Arctic demanded that they adopt the local lifestyle and diet. Hunting and fishing became as much the trader's way of life as it was for his customers.

Except for the very significant fact of the introduction (unintentional, at least on the part of the trading companies) of Old World diseases among the indigenous peoples, there is considerable evidence that the fur trade in its first phase contributed to an immediate and substantial improvement in the standard of living of the Aboriginal peoples — particularly through the use of iron, copper, and steel tools, firearms, and cookware. Another indication of the intentions of the "Honourable Company" is that in establishing each trading post the initial inventory always included a well-stocked medical kit and the Factors, the managers of the Hbc posts, were trained in its use for the benefit of the Native traders.

While there is little evidence of the trading companies being so foolishly shortsighted as to actively attempt to eliminate their own customers and suppliers, once the peoples of the First Nations began to adopt a more European diet their general health did begin to deteriorate. And by 1800, Hudson's Bay Company and its main rival, the North West Company, found themselves engaged in a heated and bitter trade war. Tragically, both companies stooped to desperate measures and alcohol unfortunately became the largest single trade item of European origin, leading to disastrous consequences for the Aboriginal peoples. Ultimately, this competition led to outright war, with the Native trappers and their families caught in the crossfire — a war that was not resolved until the two companies merged in 1821. By then, however, the days of the beaver trade were numbered. Within a few years the European taste for top hats made of beaver felt swung toward hats made of silk. While furs continued to be exported to Europe, it wasn't until the 1930s that the demand for muskrat skins for both men's and women's coats caused a new fur boom in the North.

# THE WEAVERS OF WITNEY

**G**reat changes were in store for the workers in the English woollen trades as the Industrial Revolution gradually transformed the making of blankets from loosely organized cottage-based family crafts to mill-based industrial enterprises.

What comes as a surprise to many interested in Hudson's Bay point blankets is the fact that Hbc itself never manufactured blankets at all. Hudson's Bay Company was always a trading company and never a manufacturing firm and thus, from the start of its trade in point blankets, it acquired them in wholesale lots from weaving operations in England. Nevertheless,

the role of the Company in maintaining high standards for the products it ordered cannot be ignored, particularly when often cheaply made American blankets flooded the Native trade market during the mid-nineteenth century.

In December of 1779, an initial order for five hundred pairs of "pointed" blankets of various sizes was placed by Hudson's Bay Company with the firm of Thomas Empson of Witney. For generations, the weavers of the village of Witney, Oxfordshire, produced particularly high quality woollen blankets or duffels, and had been the principal suppliers of Hudson's Bay Company's previous blanket purchases since at least 1682. The traditional process of blanket making required the skills of a variety of craftsmen; a master weaver contracting to supply blankets organized the job by contracting out the various stages to independent "piece workers."

Before the Industrial Revolution, the master weavers acquired their wool either directly from sheep farmers or from middlemen, "broggers," who dealt in raw and spun wool. Or they acquired it from "fell-mongers,"

(Below) Blanket Weavers' Hall in Witney, Oxfordshire, was built in 1721. Every blanket made in Witney was brought here to be weighed and measured before receiving the mark of approval from the Hall keepers. (Opposite) This eighteenth-century engraving illustrates the old art of wool preparation.

The first Plate of the Woollen Manufacture exhibiting the Art of (A) Sheep Shearing (B) The Washing (C) The Beating & (D) The Combing of Wool.

Engraved for the Universal Magazine 1749 for J. Hinton at the Kings Arms in St Pauls Church Yard London

dealers who bought the wool shorn from sheep slaughtered for meat in the urban marketplaces. The origin of the wool in old point blankets was principally from farms near the mills where the blankets were made. The raw wool was sorted and graded into its various types based on fibre length, texture, and character and then blended into the desired ratio for the specific type of blanket to be woven.

Before the blend of raw wool was to be carded and spun it was mixed with a certain amount of rapeseed oil and dyed. There are three methods of producing dyed wool products. The wool can be dyed prior to its being spun into yarn ("dyed in the wool"), after the wool has been spun ("dyed in the yarn"), or after the blanket is woven ("dyed in the piece"). The highest quality and therefore preferred method for Hbc's point blankets was to dye the wool prior to spinning. This yields the most even application of the dye throughout the finished blanket.

In the early years, the processes of carding ("opening" the fleece to allow more even spinning) and spinning (drawing out, twisting, and winding the wool fibres into yarn or thread) were contracted out to cottage spinners and the yarn was then collected and delivered to the weavers. Most operations were cottage-based in the seventeenth and eighteenth centuries, but as the Industrial Revolution advanced, each of the various stages of blanket manufacture was gradually transferred into factory settings, which ultimately combined into single mills that housed all stages of production.

The blankets were originally woven by hand in long continuous rolls of cloth totalling some eight or so pairs, depending on the width of the blankets being manufactured. The looms were over three yards wide and were originally operated by two weavers at a time: the

(Right) The Industrial Revolution brought about an eventual end to the craft of the handloom weaver.

(Above) A man gathers bundles of wool in the blending bin of a blanket factory in Witney.
(Opposite) This photograph from the early twentieth century shows a man working a machine that dries and folds woollen fabric in one of England's mills.

of warp threads when one set is raised is called the "shed." The weft thread is run through the shed with the use of a shuttle, a shaped block of wood carrying a "bobbin" on which the weft thread is carried and from which it is unwound into the weave. The newly laid line of weft is pushed snugly down into the forming blanket cloth with a comb-like device called a "reed." The beams rotate to take up the cloth as it is finished and feed the warp threads into the working area.

The yarn count (measured by counting the number of warp and weft yarns to the inch) determines the closeness or looseness of the weave. (A modern Hbc point blanket has about twenty weft threads to the inch.) The proportion and order of weft threads in relation to the warp threads determines the type of weave. In "plain" weave each weft thread passes over each adjacent warp thread for the full width of the cloth. On each subsequent row, the order or interlacing is alternated yielding an even checkerboard appearance. Plain weave fabrics include linen, muslin, and taffeta. A common variation of the plain weave is the "basket" weave, in which two or more weft yarns are interlaced with two or more warp yarns yielding a very loose weave, as seen in "monk's cloth" or burlap.

journeyman "throwing" the shuttle from the right and the apprentice throwing it back from the left.

To weave the cloth, two sets of threads or yarns are intertwined perpendicularly to each other. The threads that run lengthwise are called the "warp" and those running crosswise are called the "weft" or "woof." Hand looms use bars or "beams" in a frame to hold the warp threads parallel in two sets. The "heddle" is used to raise one set of the warp threads at a time and is often operated with a foot pedal. The gap created between the two groups

Traditional English-made point blankets use a "twill" weave where the weft threads are interwoven with pairs of the warp threads and are shifted by one warp thread on each subsequent throw. The result is a diagonal ribbed pattern (these ribs are called "wales") in the finished cloth. The twill weave is also used to make denim, gabardine, some tweeds, and serge.

At the very edges of a point blanket a selvage is created by picking up the pairs of warp threads without shifting from row to row of the weft, as was done in the body of the blanket's twill weave. The weaving in the selvage is properly a plain weave and creates a stronger edge since the warp is

effectively heavier in that area. The width of the selvage varied from weaver to weaver depending on how many pairs of warp threads were in the selvage and is thus a clue to identifying different runs of blankets.

Since the warp is continuous through the run of blanketing, its colour remains the same for the whole length of the blanket. However, the bars or headings are created by shifting to a different colour yarn on the bobbin for a sufficient number of throws of the shuttle. It is believed that the headings were introduced at the commencement of roll weaving to define the intended length of

each blanket on the roll. Single or multiple bar headings were woven into the blanket near the intended start and end of each finished blanket. The result was that the end heading from one blanket was about a foot to a foot and a half from the start heading of the next blanket on the roll.

The points themselves were short lengths of coarsely spun indigo or scarlet-coloured wool woven or sewn into the edge of each blanket's field to indicate the intended width of the finished blanketing. Originally, they were not standardized and each weaver used his own style of point marking. The earliest blankets show much shorter points than the finger-length ones apparent on blankets after the end of the eighteenth century. By the mid-nineteenth century, points were generally made from indigo wool and ran about four and a half inches for a full point and about two and a half inches per half point.

The black bars and points were at various times produced from wool dyed with indigo, logwood, iron-based, or "aniline fast" dyes. To replace indigo, which was often difficult to acquire and expensive to use, logwood dyes were used during the mid-nineteenth century. Logwood (*Haematoxylon campechianum*), derived from a tree native to the West Indies and the Yucatan Peninsula, can be used to produce a deep purple

depending on the mordant or agent used to fix the dye to the wool fibres. During the First World War guaranteed-fast aniline dyes were in use to produce the blue-black bars and points. But the colour was comparatively flat and unattractive; so much so, that in 1923 the staff of Hudson's Bay Company were instructed to state in future press releases that from that date on all new blankets would only be manufactured using pure indigo dyes.

Once woven, the whole roll of blanketing would be unloaded from the take-up side of the loom and turned over to the "tuckers" for "fulling." A finished roll of blanketing might run some 150 feet in length and weigh around 75 to 100 pounds. Blankets intended to be six feet in width were actually woven as a loose coarse cloth almost nine feet wide. At this stage the loosely woven cloth, not unlike burlap in texture and looseness of weave, was scoured to remove the added oils, soaked in water and fuller's earth (an absorbent claylike substance), and then pounded to shrink the cloth to the specific proper width for the size of blankets being made. The process of fulling causes the blanket to shrink and "felt" slightly, giving the English-made point blanket its particularly dense, high insulating characteristic.

# MAKING TODAY'S BLANKET

**A**lthough modern technology has revolutionized the production of textiles such as the Hudson's Bay point blanket, the various stages in the process are virtually the same as in the days of the cottage industries. Today, wool has to be ordered several months in advance to ensure that the correct grades are available to meet production demand.

### WOOL STORING

Bales of raw wool from carefully selected suppliers in England and New Zealand are stored in the warehouse until needed.

### BLENDING

After the locks of wool are "opened" by a special machine, the different types of wool are thoroughly mixed in the right proportions and oil is added to facilitate spinning.

### CARDING

The wool fibres are straightened or "carded" and any loose debris is removed by passing them over a series of large spiked rollers before they are formed into long strands called "slivers" ready for spinning into yarn.

### SPINNING

Modern spinning machines have replaced the old "mule" frames, which were used until recently for certain yarns. These impart the "twist" and elongation in the yarn for strength. Yarns of different thickness are used for the warp and weft.

### WINDING

After spinning, the finished yarn is wound onto cones of the correct size and shape for use in the looms and for producing the warp.

### WARPING

Warps comprising up to 2,600 threads across and up to 74 yards in length are produced in sections on large rollers known as the warping mill, swift, or balloon before being wound onto beams and transported to the looms.

## WEAVING

Modern rapier looms up to 12 feet wide are used to weave Hudson's Bay point blankets.

## WEAVING/WEFT

Mechanisms called "dobbies," controlled by punch tape, bring in the coloured weft yarns when required to weave the distinctive Hudson's Bay stripes. The short indigo points are also woven in the loom using thicker yarn.

## PICKING

"Picking" refers to the skilled job of removing any knots and flaws and mending any other faults in the woven pieces. The cloth is thoroughly inspected, measured, and weighed.

## SHAVING

The loose ends of yarn from producing the tucked selvages are shaved off to produce a smooth edge.

## SCOURING AND MILLING

The cloth is "scoured" or washed in mild detergent to remove any remaining oil. "Milling," the action of running the pieces through rollers, closes up the woven fabric and reduces the width of the piece giving it density and stability.

## RAISING

The blankets are brushed with fine wire rollers to lift the pile or nap giving the texture, warmth, and good looks for which Hudson's Bay point blankets are famous. The blankets are inspected and weighed before they are torn by hand into individual blankets, the points brushed by hand, and the labels sewn on.

In 1800, a blanket
factory had a vat
under the men's
washroom to
collect urine to
be used, much
like astringent,
to remove oils
from the woollen
cloth before it
was dyed. Today,
a mixture of
soda and mild
soap is used.

.

Once the "stockful," the roll of blanketing, was shrunken and felted, it was hung to dry on long outdoor racks in the sun. Sun drying served to set the dyes and, in the case of the common white field blankets, actually bleached them to the bright white preferred by Native Americans. To create a raised nap, giving the point blankets their characteristic soft texture and warmth, the dried blanketing was "rowed" by the tuckers who originally used teasels, a finely bristled plant, as the means of catching the wool fibres and raising them.

The actual dimensions of a blanket, especially in the case of a hand-woven one, will vary slightly from the standard indicated by the number of points. This is due to the fact that the process of manufacturing involves a stage of shrinkage or felting. Variations in temperature, soaking time, and fulling can lead to variations in the finished size of the blanket. Later handling and cleaning of blankets can cause further shrinkage. Accordingly, expecting an older three and half-point blanket to be exactly 63 inches in width is unrealistic. Even when it was originally sold it could be as narrow as 61 inches or as wide as 65 inches. For shipping, the long roll was cut down (actually torn) into pairs of blankets. A manageable number of folded pairs was stacked and sewn into canvas or burlap bales and transported by ship to North America and then on by canoe or York Boat to the remote trading posts of the British North American interior.

With the invention of the "fly-shuttle" in 1733, the blanket industry commenced the slow process of industrialization. Initially the weavers resisted all such "advances." The fly-shuttle, for instance, made it possible for a single weaver to throw the shuttle from side to side with the use of mechanical "hands." At first, the introduction of this innovation appeared to threaten the displacement of half of the weaving work force. But since the demand for blankets for the North American trade was growing rapidly, this advance made it possible for the same number of weavers to produce twice as many blankets, and in fact led to an increase in individual earning power.

Until about 1840, the Witney blanket weavers nearly monopolized the manufacture of point blankets for Hudson's Bay Company. So much so, that for many years pointed blankets were also called "Witney" blankets, as the Company ordered blankets in ever increasing quantities from the Oxford-based mills operated by the Empson, Marriot, and Early families. By the peak of the fur trade, in the early nineteenth century, Hbc had such a high demand for point blankets that it concurrently ordered blankets from a number of different weaving companies throughout central and northern England. Several companies in the Calder Valley district, centred in the Dewsbury, Yorkshire, area are known to have supplied Hbc with blankets during the mid-nineteenth century, including Atkinson, Brush and Co.; William Atkinson and Co.; Hagues, Cook & Wormald; Alexander & Henry Co.; Thomas Long; and Horatio W. Collier & Sons. This diversity of originating mills is reflected in many of the variations in the details of blankets being marketed at any one time by Hudson's Bay Company.

Although mechanization was introduced gradually throughout the eighteenth and nineteenth centuries, so that now most of the processes are carried out on machines, the underlying methods of manufacture today remain fundamentally the same as those used in handweaving. The massive modern looms have allowed the manufacture of much longer rolls of blankets and, in 1929, when Hbc introduced a line of pastel-coloured point blankets, it was necessary to dye this specific line "in the piece" rather than "in the wool."

## MAKING THE TRADITIONAL COAT

Manufactured in Winnipeg, Manitoba, the line of garments made from the point blanket cloth includes jackets and coats for both men and women. But the Hbc Traditional Coat — particularly the one made of multistripe cloth — remains the most popular. In the first three photographs at left, the various pieces of a blanket coat are prepared for sewing (bottom).

# MORE THAN JUST A BLANKET

(Right) Ceremoniously draping his point blanket over his shoulder, the Red Lake chief makes a speech to the governor of Red River at Fort Douglas in 1825.

Until about 1880, the majority of point blankets shipped from England to British North America, as well as the vast output from the Eastern American mills, were intended for use by Native Canadians and Americans. But for these Aboriginal peoples the blanket was no mundane utilitarian household item. Nor was the blanket a newly introduced cultural artifact. In fact, blankets made from hides, woven plant fibres, or even native wools had existed in North America prior to the introduction of European-made woollen trade goods. For most of the indigenous peoples the blanket served as the outer layer of clothing and as such reflected the style choices of its wearer. And, like the togas of the Roman aristocracy, blankets served as "props," illustrative of the wearer's mood or oratorical attitude. The way in which a robe was draped over the body could be quite stylized and by convention could signify certain emotional states in support of the wearer's argument. The particular attraction of European wool blankets was their high insulating character in relation to their weight, their suppleness, and their availability in strong, vibrant colours.

Point blankets always came in a variety of colours and sizes. A common error that dates back to the early nineteenth century is to refer to the "traditional" white blankets with stripes of several different colours, wherever it was made or whoever marketed it, as a "Hudson's Bay" or "chief's" blanket. More correctly these blankets are called "multistripes." It is unclear whether

Hudson's Bay Company offered multistripes much before the early 1800s and today's well-known pattern of the multistripe — indigo, yellow, red, and green — did not always follow this colour order. It wasn't until the late nineteenth century that the pattern was standardized by the Company. There has been considerable speculation that the colours and their order in the multistripe have some hidden or cultural meaning for the native buyers. It is more likely, however, that the selection of colours was based on the early availability of four particularly strong primary coloured dyes.

Hudson's Bay point blankets have been made available over the years in sizes ranging from as small as the very rare early one-point (at approximately three by four feet) to the comparatively recent introduction of the king-sized eight-point blanket (at 100 by 108 inches). In the early eighteenth century, blanket sales at Fort Niagara were predominantly two points in size, each blanket measuring approximately four by five feet and weighing around three and one half pounds, which reflects their principal use as wearing rather than sleeping robes. But most commonly,

TEN CENTS PER COPY

The Beaver

No. 3    OUTFIT 261    DEC. 1930

Hudson's Bay Company
INCORPORATED 2ND MAY 1670

throughout the nineteenth century, blankets were marketed in the three-point/four pound, three and a half-point/five pound, and four-point/six pound sizes. Again, the points are purely an indication of the size or area of a blanket, with the weight varying accordingly. The actual cloth from a manufacturer was of the same

width of the blankets usually were in even multiples of a quarter yard, or nine inches. In the cloth manufacturing trade, blanket sizes were identified by their width in quarter yards, thus an "8/4" was eight quarters of a yard wide (e.g., 72 inches), typical for a four-point blanket then and now. The proportions might vary somewhat on the basis of the ultimate purpose of the blanket, but they usually appear to reflect the practical ratio of the length averaging around one and a quarter times the width.

Point assignment was not absolutely standard from manufacturer to manufacturer and, because of the nature of the shrinkage process, they were really more an approximation of the intended standard size. The variety of sizes available at any given time indicates the various uses the blankets were put to. A four-point blanket at 72 inches in width would be too long to wear as a robe, while a three point at only 72 inches in length would be too short for an adult to sleep under, but would make an ample wearing robe for a man.

thickness or weight per square yard whatever the number of points, as long as the runs were of the same grade. On the average, a full point represented about a yard (nine square feet) of finished cloth, with less area per point in the smaller blankets and more in the higher point sizes. This, of course, reflected the added unit costs of manufacturing and handling smaller items of trade. The length and the

(Opposite) While a three-point blanket could make an ample wearing robe, such as the one worn by this Aboriginal man photographed in Winnipeg in 1881, a four-point blanket had more than enough cloth to fashion a child's coat, such as the one shown in this 1922 ad (right).

# Hudson's Bay Company

*For* Service Value, H.B.C. "Point" Blankets are Unparalleled

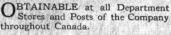

OBTAINABLE at all Department Stores and Posts of the Company throughout Canada.

*STANDARD PRICES:*
4 point Size—72 x 90 in., $13.00 pr.
3½ point Size—63 x 80 in., $12.50 pr.
3 point Size—61 x 74 in., $10.50 pr.

**NONE GENUINE WITHOUT THE SEAL OF QUALITY.**

THE "LITTLE TRAPPER" WEARS A WARM COAT MADE FROM A 4-POINT BLANKET

## STRIPES, COLOURS, AND SASHES

**P**oint blankets were traditionally made in plain red, white, green, or blue fields with single bars of deep indigo or black near each end. For varying reasons, the multistriped pattern was not as attractive to the traditional Canadian tribes as these plainer colourations. The Plains hunters preferred the simple white blankets, which they made into coats or "capotes" that provided camouflage in winter. But for the Plains Indians the preference for white may also have had a spiritual basis.

Among the coastal tribes of the Pacific Northwest, the Tsimshian and Tlingit preferred deep blue, while to the south along the west coast of Canada, the Kwakiutl and Nuu-Cha-Nuth favoured green blankets. Red blankets, popular among the Coast and Interior Salish, also appealed to non-Native people living in the bush — making them the most commonly found older blankets after the pure white and multistripe. The Métis — the peoples descended from intermarriage between Scottish traders, French voyageurs, and the

*ne*—Continued varied—scarlet, green, yellow, blue, and beige.
and blue for heels on men's shoes and as a stocking color. Black

appeared and yellow maintained its popularity.
lors worn at once—petticoat, dress, and cloak. Little taste shown.

(Above) Fashion historians refer to the four colours (green, red, yellow, and indigo) of the multistripe blanket as "Queen Anne's colours" — tones that became popular during that monarch's reign (1700–1714). The appeal of these colours is still so strong that Hbc now uses them as part of its corporate identity. (Opposite top) Several Métis are visible wearing multistripe blankets or coats, with and without a colourful sash, in this depiction of Louis Riel and Donald A. Smith addressing the crowd at Fort Garry in 1870. (Opposite bottom) A white blanket and point blanket coat offer this trapper and his wife some camouflage as well as warmth.

Native peoples of the Canadian West — were partial to the multistripe, reflecting their leaning toward colourful textiles.

This taste is also apparent in their use of the *Assomption* sash — a colourful, four-yard-long woven textile originating in Quebec, which, in later years, was also marketed by Hudson's Bay Company. All of these general preferences, however, were not absolute; in fact, most colours were traded in most areas throughout Canada's West and North.

# THE BLANKET
# GOES WEST

**P**oint blankets were not only a standard item of trade, they were also one of the principal treaty benefits due to the Native peoples from the governments of the United States and newly formed Canada. In 1870, three years after Canadian Confederation, all the lands previously administered by Hudson's Bay Company, known as Rupert's Land, were transferred to Canada and formed the Northwest Territories. Throughout this process a number of treaties were negotiated with many (but not all) of the indigenous nations of the Canadian West and the North. To induce the peoples of the First Nations to give up title to their lands, their leaders were compelled to sign treaties with promises of land reserved for the people's sole use, legal recognition of their traditional hunting and fishing rights, and the promise of certain treaty benefits to be paid annually. These "annuity" benefits included farming equipment, livestock, medical and education services, a small amount of cash, and blankets for every man, woman, and child.

A Blackfoot First Nations man wearing an Hbc blanket coat stands in front of a Catholic mission on a reserve in 1881.

(Left) Point blankets destined for a potlatch are piled against Kwakiutl Indian House at Fort Rupert in 1898. (Above) The Anglican Rev. Timms and his wife pose with a group of Blackfoot First Nations members in this photograph from 1887 taken in front of a mission in Alberta. (Right) An 1881 ledger drawing from a Blackfoot reserve clearly shows a Native man wearing a point blanket coat.

## THE CAPOTE

**B**y the end of the 1870s, the Blackfoot First Nations seamstresses adapted the old French capote style — a plain white blanket with a single indigo stripe above the bottom edge. They fashioned versions of the coats that included fringes or tassels on the hood, shoulder seams, or cuffs (left), and bead, fur, or hair embellishments on the shoulders, sleeves, or upper coat body, and red wool seam binding. Sometimes the Hbc label was prominently displayed on the outside lower front flap of the coat, particularly on the multistriped coats made after 1900. (Right) The capotes were usually worn closed with a decorated or plain leather gun belt, a pouch, a knife and/or gun and scabbard, blanket leggings, moccasins, or boots, and individual headgear (perhaps a Stetson or a ceremonial headdress). This meaningful ensemble was worn at government, society, and tribal meetings, as well as at sundances, pow wows, and other summer festivals. After more than 130 years, the blanket coats of the Blackfoot First Nations continue to be made and worn with pride.

By the end of the nineteenth century, most blankets acquired by the Native peoples of the prairies were from treaty payments and not earned from the trade in furs. No longer were Europeans satisfied with the mere fruits of the land, such as furs and castoreum, and "annuity blankets" became one of the principal items used as "payment" for title to the very lands of the peoples of the West. Thus, an era came to an end.

As the treaties were being negotiated, the Canadian and American West was opened to non-Native settlement, and with that settlement, gradually the Canadian North itself was penetrated by prospectors and adventurers seeking wealth based on resources other than those derived from furs. Many of these new Northerners wisely adopted the survival strategies of the Native peoples. And for them the point blanket was every bit as useful as it had been for the indigenous people of the region. While these new "bushmen" may not have shared the Native user's attitude toward the social and spiritual significance of the point blanket, they did find them to be a "raw" material with value beyond that of simple bedding. A point blanket could be shaped into a robe, a capote or long hooded coat, and a vest; cut up to make breeches or leggings; or formed into boot

(Right) Five of the nine Blackfoot men seated in front of the whitewashed wall of Hbc's Rocky Mountain House trading post in 1871 are wearing point blanket coats.

tops, liners, or even socks. Its great insulating capacity made it suitable to form a door for a cabin, a roof for a lean-to, or the bedding on a dog sled. There are numerous stories of Hudson's Bay point blankets being used as shrouds for the dead, a blanket for a newborn baby, a patch for a boat's hull, or even a sail for a canoe.

**B**y 1900, with the great Klondike Gold Rush, the shift from Native to non-Native users had reached the point that the majority of Hbc's sales of point blankets was no longer made to the "Indian" trade. And through the early years of the twentieth century new markets developed for point blankets as Canada rapidly urbanized. City-dwelling sportsmen discovered the advantages of these blankets as they came in contact with full-time residents of the Northern bush. Endorsed by adventurers and explorers, the point blanket became the bedding of choice before the advent of lightweight goose down sleeping bags. Hudson's Bay point blankets were used on expeditions to both poles, the "conquest" of Everest, and on Lindbergh's famed transatlantic flights.

WE HAVE HEARD—

—OF MANY STRANGE USES FOR OUR BLANKETS

FROM washing for gold, getting cars out of mud holes, and covering a precious stock of potatoes, to one blanket which has had six Indian babies born on it. But the strangest use is the one pictured above - a sail for an Eskimo "ice schooner." All these strange and strenuous uses seem to prove just one thing—if you need a blanket which will wear, wear again, and then outwear you, buy a Hudson's Bay "Point" Blanket.

**Hudson's Bay Company.**
INCORPORATED 2ND MAY 1670.

(Opposite) There are unusual stories of the uses of Hbc point blankets, including this one of the blanket being used as a sail on a sled in the Arctic — a story that was picked up for an ad in the June 1934 issue of Hbc's *The Beaver.* (Right) A colour ad from the 1956 winter issue of the same magazine highlights the blanket's use on Antarctic and Mount Everest expeditions.

*With* Byrd to the Antarctic . . . .

## Hudson's Bay point Blankets

**famous the world over for a lifetime of luxurious comfort and warmth.**

*With* climbing expeditions to Everest . . .

# FINDING NEW MARKETS

Vacationing "at the cottage" is an especially Canadian phenomenon. Perhaps nowhere else in the world has a nation's urban residents had such ready access to vast tracts of wilderness. With a land area to population ratio approximately fifteen times that of the United States, it should be no surprise that even working class families in Canada were capable of owning a small acreage within a few hours journey of their homes in Toronto, Montreal, or Winnipeg. Initially, their easily afforded "tent cabins" served as the base camp for fall sport hunting by the men of the family. But in time, as logs or planks replaced canvas walls, "the cottage at the lake" became the annual summer refuge for the whole family. It is likely that every such cottage had at least one point blanket purchased from Hbc. And, when the variety of colours and patterns available was expanded in 1929, it was a short leap for a point blanket to become part of the décor of the family's principal residence back in the city.

North American hunters and campers saw the benefits of the warmth and durability of Hbc point blankets as this painting (opposite), reproduced on the November 1921 cover of *The Beaver* (right), vividly illustrates.

For decades, American tourists visiting Canada bought "Hudson's Bay Blankets" as practical souvenirs of their holiday, since blankets of such quality and with such a special pedigree were not readily available south of the border.

Vol. II    NOVEMBER, 1921    No. 2

The Beaver

A Journal of Progress

HBC

UNLOADED!

Devoted to The Interests of Those Who Serve The Hudson's Bay Company

Admittedly, Hudson's Bay Company point blankets had worked their way south into the United States, primarily through exchange among members of the Indian tribes straddling the border like the Niitsitapii (Blackfoot), the Stó:lo (Salish), and the Ktunaxa (Kootenay) in the West. But as mainstream middle-class interest in these blankets rose, Hudson's Bay Company began to actively market them into the United States. Since the 1920s, the L.L. Bean Company of Freeport, Maine, had been offering Hudson's Bay point blankets primarily to sportsmen. By 1928, a wholly owned subsidiary, Hudson's Bay Company, Inc., had offices at 165 Broadway in New York City and acted as its own United States sales agent for blankets and the other unique products of the Company. Today, Pearce Woolen Mills, a subsidiary of Woolrich, Inc., represents the Hudson's Bay point blanket trade in the United States.

The 1910–11 Hudson's Bay Company mail order catalogue offered three sizes of point blanket in four colours: red, green, navy blue, and white. During the First World War, khaki and grey blankets were also available, but were of slightly lower quality and cost. Around 1920, as the market for point blankets shifted from principally Aboriginal and other "bush" users to cottagers and middle-class homeowners, the colour preference trend changed and the multistripe became by far the most popular style, while the plain white blanket with black bars was discontinued around 1940.

(Opposite) For "home, camp, or trail," nothing could beat the quality of an Hbc point blanket, and the multistripe as seen in this ad (below) became the most popular blanket style.

Let go of MY BLANKET

One of his most prized possessions is that HUDSON'S BAY Point BLANKET

It's something he won't grow out of but grow up with. On those future camping expeditions and canoe trips, he'll find it the same perfect companion as now— warm and dependable —cosy and colourful.

BEFORE YOU BUY—LOOK FOR THIS LABEL ON ALL GENUINE HUDSON'S BAY "POINT" BLANKETS

# BLANKETS

This 1939 Saskatoon store display shows the range of blanket types and colours offered by the Company.

But during that same period Hudson's Bay Company also issued a new series of colours: the Pastel Tones were a successful new line offering "modern decorator" colours and were first offered in 1929.

By the middle of the Great Depression, Hbc had added two more new lines called the Imperial Tones and Deep Tones. The Imperial Tones, and specifically the Coronation blanket, in royal blue with red headings and points, were issued to commemorate the intended coronation of King Edward VIII. With the King's abdication before his formal coronation, this blanket is more commonly associated with the coronation of George VI in 1937. It was revived in 1953 for the coronation of Queen Elizabeth II (who ascended to the throne in 1952), but at this point was produced in a royal purple with white bars and points.

In later years, a few additional pastel toned blankets were introduced, like "Tango" (orange) and "Sunshine" (yellow), but the popularity of the Pastels, Deep, and

In the 1930s, the range of blanket colours expanded to include the Pastel, Imperial, and Deep Tones.

**Hudson's Bay Company.**

INCORPORATED 2ᴺᴰ MAY 1670.

**The Ideal Christmas Gift!**

HUDSON'S BAY "POINT" BLANKETS

IN

NEW PASTEL SHADES

ROSE    SKYBLUE    HELIO
GOLD    RESEDA

On sale at all Hudson's Bay Company stores: Winnipeg (Man.); Saskatoon, Yorkton (Sask.); Calgary, Edmonton, Lethbridge (Alta.); Vancouver, Victoria, Kamloops, Nelson, Vernon (B.C.); and at the Company's Fur Trade posts throughout Canada.

# A BLANKET FIT FOR ROYALTY

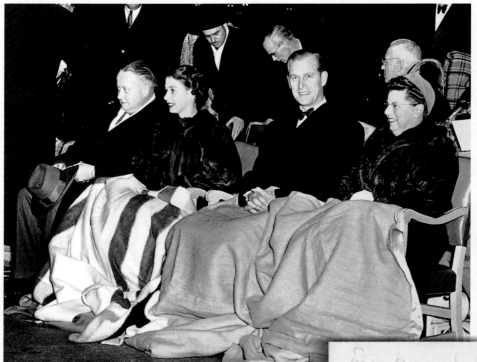

The point blanket and coat have an illustrious royal history. (Above) Hudson's Bay point blankets warmed Princess Elizabeth and the Duke of Edinburgh in Edmonton, Alberta, during their 1951 Royal Visit to Canada. The Coronation blanket, as seen in this advertisement (right), was revived in 1953 in honour of Queen Elizabeth II's coronation and featured a royal purple field with white bars and points. A Hudson's Bay blanket coat was presented to Prince Charles in July 1977 following his ceremonial induction as an honourary Chief of the Kainai Chieftanship Society of the Blood Tribe in southern Alberta.

... in Royal Colour

Elizabeth R
1953

The Coronation

HUDSON'S BAY
POINT BLANKET

for a lifetime
of comfort
and warmth

Imperial Tones waned during the 1960s and only a few of these nontraditional colours remained available. When these lines were discontinued around 1970, the traditional plain reds, blues, greens, and multistripes were all that remained on the market.

In 1999, the Bay announced two new patterns: one a reintroduction of the traditional grey with black stripes last available around 1920, and a whole new multistripe in muted natural browns and greys, to commemorate the new millennium. To celebrate the Company's 330th anniversary, 330 two-point "Millennium" blankets were produced to be awarded to associates who successfully answered an Hbc trivia contest. In 2001, a limited issue of the old standard white with indigo bars was produced primarily for use by museums and in capote-making workshops.

As the selection of colours was broadened to appeal to a wider market, so too the variety of sizes available was modified and expanded as the Hudson's Bay point blanket found its way into urban homes. For instance, around 1970 the old three-and-a-half-point standard changed from 63 inches by 81 inches to 60 by 86 inches to more effectively accommodate a modern "single" bed; and in 1997 the two-point blanket standard was changed from 54 by 72 inches to 50 by 60 inches at the request of the Woolrich Company, the United States importer of Hbc's point blankets. It was felt that there would be more of a market for a throw than for the traditional crib blanket. The former size, which was originally intended for use as a child's wearing robe had been discontinued during the early 1980s. Again, it is worth noting that the older sizes in both cases still reflected the over 400-year-old weaver's convention of standard dimensions based on multiples of a quarter of a yard.

Such size changes generally reflected accommodation to more modern mattress types; and, as the standard sizes of beds increased, the range of point blanket sizes expanded. In the late 1960s a new six-point queen-sized blanket was offered at 90 by 100 inches; and again in the early 1980s the Bay introduced the huge eight-point king-sized blanket at 100 by 108 inches (later lengthened to 110 inches).

The Millennium blanket (above) is featured on the front of a blanket brochure.

While sizes and colours have been changed to reflect shifts in consumer demand and taste, more subtle changes in the weave and finish of the blankets have been made from time to time. For instance, the length of the nap on 1930s blankets was quite shaggy and significantly greater than that on modern blankets, while the grey and khaki blankets from the turn of the twentieth century had virtually no nap at all.

Although First Nations and bush users throughout the nineteenth century had modified point blankets into a variety of different articles of clothing — most famously, the capote — it wasn't until just before 1930 that the Company started to introduce a broad line of sportswear "ready made" from point blanket cloth. In 1930, Hbc offered double and single-breasted overcoats with and without hoods, caps, and toques in matching colours, as well as windbreakers and dressing gowns. And by the mid-1930s, the line had expanded to include mid-length car coats, fashionable dress coats, casual sportswear, mittens, berets, peaked caps, scarves, and stylish cadet caps for ladies. Most of these were available in both the traditional and new pastel colours, and the line and styles continued to expand and

The point blanket's popularity as a bed cover (below right) was the impetus for size changes in the 1960s to fit queen-sized beds (below left) and later in the 1980s for king-sized beds.

HUDSON'S BAY *Point* BLANKETS

A Generous Queen Size 6 Point Blanket!

Keyed to today's Luxury Living—the superb quality of Hudson's Bay Point Blankets now provides you the same warm comfort and lasting service in a generous Queen size—90" x 100". You'll welcome the all-round tuck in the 6-point affords on your Queen size bed. Specially loomed in England to Hudson's Bay standards of Quality and finished with the same skill and care which has made Hudson's Bay Point Blankets a Standard for the World for almost 2 centuries. Colors: Rose, Gold, Multi-stripe, Sky Blue.

Hudson's Bay Company INCORPORATED 2ND MAY 1670 BLANKET DIVISION *(and Leisure Wear)*

evolve over the years in keeping with changing fashion trends.

These changes in markets for the Hudson's Bay point blankets were reflected by modifications in how they were shipped and packaged. Over the years, most references to the purchase and sale of point blankets itemize them in "pairs." As late as the 1960s, Hudson's Bay Company advertising gave the weights and prices of their blankets in pairs, although the dimensions usually cited are for single blankets. A pair of blankets was generally unseparated until after sale, if at all. It has been claimed that this convention arises from the peculiarities of American customs practices that levied duties on the basis of single pieces of wool items. But the more likely reasons for this practice reflect the ultimate uses of the blankets and the traditional methods of manufacturing and shipping them.

Quintin Finlay, who joined the Company in the 1950s and is the former manager of Hudson's Bay Company's and North West Company's blanket divisions, notes that the blankets still arrived in bales

In the 1930s, the Company introduced a broad range of sportswear made from point blanket cloth, including men's and ladies' jacket styles and full-length ladies' coats.

of pairs up to 1973. To minimize their bulky volume during shipping from England, the blankets were placed in a press and compressed before being sewn into jute sacking, or burlap, and bound with rope. The three-and-a-half-point blankets were packed 25 pairs per bale and the four-point twenty pairs to the bale. Finlay recalls that handling 240 to 250 pound bales by hand before the availability of forklifts was a mighty task. And contrary to popular opinion, unlike the fur bales, the blanket bales did not bear seals.

Stocked on the shelves of trading posts and the Bay's urban department stores, the blankets were available to the buyer as unseparated pairs or singles. To create two singles, the blanket pair was not cut apart. Rather, a small cut with a knife or scissors was made in the selvage at the halfway point in the pair's length and then the two halves were torn apart. This insured that they separated along a line of the weave so that their ends would not unravel once they were split apart. Finlay remembers with considerable relish the look of shock on uninitiated customers' faces when he would dramatically tear a blanket pair in half to produce two singles for them.

In the United States from sometime after World War II until 1996, the blankets were split into singles and packaged to be sold in long, attractive cardboard boxes. Inside the lid of the box was a brief summary of the history of the Hudson's Bay point blanket and the fur trade. In Canada during this period, the blankets were packed into individual plastic bags. Unfortunately, on the shelf the bags slipped about and made an unsightly mess of the displays. To deal with this problem, Hudson's Bay Company adopted a carton for its Canadian sales and in 1977 received the Canadian Carton of the Year Award in the Canadian Industry Design Competition for the new gift box. This packaging, sporting a colourful fur trade themed image, was designed by Gordon W. Wallace, manufactured by Larson Packaging of Scarborough, Ontario, and was used until about 1988.

But after all the effort to make such a high quality product, the packing into bales compressed the blanket so much that it crushed its carefully raised nap and thus did not show off the blanket's high loft. In 1984, at Quintin Finlay's insistence, the modern practice of individually packaging the blankets in vinyl zip bags in England before shipping was instituted. In 1996 the U.S. wholesaler adopted the same bags and retired its use of cardboard boxes.

(Below) This U.S. wholesaler's box received an honourable mention in the 1939 All-American Package Competition.

# THE WORTH OF A BLANKET

For many years, Hudson's Bay point blankets, when not directly exchanged in trade for furs, were sold purely by weight, at nearly the same price per pound whatever the point size. In 1800, a four-point blanket pair sold for about £2, then the equivalent of about US$10, or around 83 cents a pound. Despite inflation, the prices remained nearly constant throughout the nineteenth century, and at times even declined. The cost-reducing effects of the Industrial Revolution combined with increasing competition from other retailers served to offset the impact of inflation on blanket prices. By about 1900, point blankets were commonly trading in Canada at one Canadian dollar per pound. This peak price was probably caused in part by the effect of great demand arising from the Klondike Gold Rush of 1897, when over 30,000 men set off for the gold fields of the Yukon Territory, each carrying a pair of point blankets in his kit. By this time the full cost benefits of industrialization and competition were in place and the prices commenced to rise steadily thereafter.

By the mid-1930s, the price had risen to approximately $22 for a pair of four-point blankets, nearly two dollars per pound, a rise of 100 percent in 40 years. These price increases apparently were triggered by rapidly rising costs of wool worldwide. And, by 1956, their price had risen to about $25 for a single four-point blanket or four dollars per pound, a rise of yet another 100 percent in twenty years. Over the next 40 years the prices have risen another 600 percent! Today, a modern four-point blanket costs about Cdn $300, around $50 per pound.

In 1800, the traditional one point to one made beaver was a workable convention. But by the 1950s, when a four-point blanket ran $25, a full-sized beaver pelt brought $24 to $30. Since a four-point blanket once equalled four made beaver, it is apparent that by this date the correlation was far out of line. And in the mid-1940s, beaver had commanded even twice as much. But, curiously, current fur prices for beaver and the retail prices for blankets more closely illustrate the traditional one "made beaver" per point correlation. At a recent auction in the United States, prime beaver pelts sold for as high as $42 each. At the same time new four-point Hudson's Bay blankets sold in the United States for about US$200 each at retail.

(Opposite) Two brochure advertisements list the various prices of the Deep Tones and Pastels (top) and the Standard Whites, Crib Blankets, and Imperial Tones (bottom).

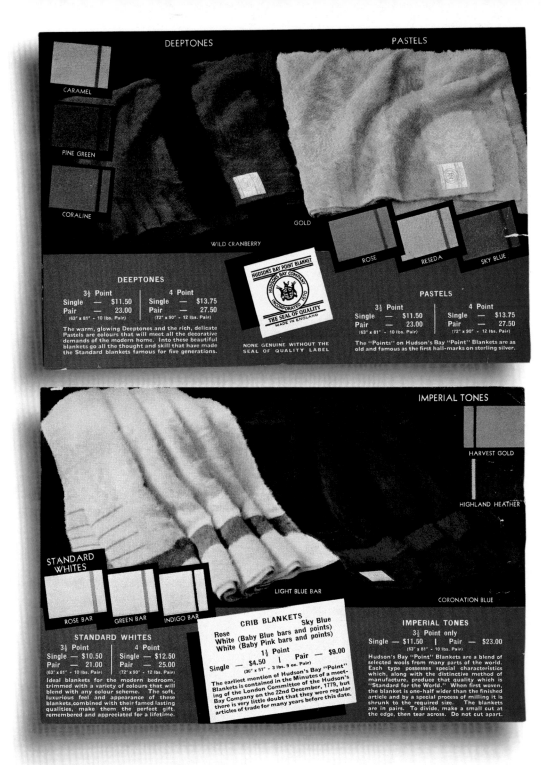

DEEPTONES    PASTELS

CARAMEL

PINE GREEN

CORALINE

WILD CRANBERRY

GOLD    ROSE    RESEDA    SKY BLUE

HUDSON'S BAY POINT BLANKET
HUDSON'S BAY COMPANY
INCORPORATED 1670
THE SEAL OF QUALITY
MADE IN ENGLAND

NONE GENUINE WITHOUT THE
SEAL OF QUALITY LABEL

## DEEPTONES

| 3½ Point | 4 Point |
|---|---|
| Single — $11.50 | Single — $13.75 |
| Pair — 23.00 | Pair — 27.50 |
| (63" x 81" - 10 lbs. Pair) | (72" x 90" - 12 lbs. Pair) |

The warm, glowing Deeptones and the rich, delicate Pastels are colours that will meet all the decorative demands of the modern home. Into these beautiful blankets go all the thought and skill that have made the Standard blankets famous for five generations.

## PASTELS

| 3½ Point | 4 Point |
|---|---|
| Single — $11.50 | Single — $13.75 |
| Pair — 23.00 | Pair — 27.50 |
| (63" x 81" - 10 lbs. Pair) | (72" x 90" - 12 lbs. Pair) |

The "Points" on Hudson's Bay "Point" Blankets are as old and famous as the first hall-marks on sterling silver.

IMPERIAL TONES

HARVEST GOLD

HIGHLAND HEATHER

CORONATION BLUE

STANDARD WHITES

ROSE BAR    GREEN BAR    INDIGO BAR

LIGHT BLUE BAR

## STANDARD WHITES

| 3½ Point | 4 Point |
|---|---|
| Single — $10.50 | Single — $12.50 |
| Pair — 21.00 | Pair — 25.00 |
| (63" x 81" - 10 lbs. Pair) | (72" x 90" - 12 lbs. Pair) |

Ideal blankets for the modern bedroom, trimmed with a variety of colours that will blend with any colour scheme. The soft, luxurious feel and appearance of these blankets, combined with their famed lasting qualities, make them the perfect gift, remembered and appreciated for a lifetime.

## CRIB BLANKETS

Rose                    Sky Blue
White (Baby Blue bars and points)
White (Baby Pink bars and points)

1½ Point
Single — $4.50    |    Pair — $9.00
(36" x 51" - 3 lbs. 9 oz. Pair)

The earliest mention of Hudson's Bay "Point" Blankets is contained in the Minutes of a meeting of the London Committee of the Hudson's Bay Company on the 22nd December, 1779, but there is very little doubt that they were regular articles of trade for many years before this date.

## IMPERIAL TONES

3½ Point only
Single — $11.50  |  Pair — $23.00
(63" x 81" - 10 lbs. Pair)

Hudson's Bay "Point" Blankets are a blend of selected wools from many parts of the world. Each type possesses special characteristics which, along with the distinctive method of manufacture, produce that quality which is "Standard for the World." When first woven, the blanket is one-half wider than the finished article and by a special process of milling it is shrunk to the required size. The blankets are in pairs. To divide, make a small cut at the edge, then tear across. Do not cut apart.

## THE BLANKET GOES TO HOLLYWOOD

**T**he story of Hudson's Bay Company was a natural for Hollywood — a saga that involved kings, lords, and trappers and unfolded amidst the untamed wilderness of North America. Hbc gave official sanction to 20th Century-Fox's production *Hudson's Bay*, starring Paul Muni as the explorer Radisson, Vincent Price in a cameo role as Charles II, and Gene Tierney as the love interest.

When the movie premiered in January 1941, store displays promoted both the film and Hudson's Bay point blankets (below). Stars of the motion picture, Paul Muni (top), Paul Sutton (middle), and Gene Tierney (opposite) pose with their blankets, gifts from Hbc.

Other Hollywood celebrities have been the recipients of Hbc blankets or coats. (Bottom) Glamorous leading lady Alexis Smith (*Gentleman Jim; Night and Day; Conflict;* and *Rhapsody in Blue*) received a full-length Hbc blanket coat in 1949. (Below) In 1958, Owen Funnell, manager of the Hbc Calgary store, presented multistriped point blankets to the Cisco Kid and Black Jack. And in the 1986 television miniseries *Dream West*, movie and television star Richard Chamberlain wore the Hbc blanket coat as the famous American explorer John Charles Fremont.

# WHAT THE LABELS MEAN

For the last hundred years or so, Hudson's Bay Company has affixed a label to each of its blankets to assure the purchaser of its genuine origin. Lacking such a label, it is difficult to identify a late nineteenth century point blanket with certainty as a Hudson's Bay point blanket, even if it meets all of the manufacturing standards established by Hbc. Since independent mills manufactured the blankets sold by the Company, identical pieces might be sold or retailed by a number of other trading companies and stores ordering from the same manufacturer. This practice became common when the Early Company of Witney started marketing "Genuine Indian Point Blankets" in Winnipeg in 1878 and were followed by retailers, like the Toronto-based T. Eaton Company, which offered competitively priced point blankets. In the late nineteenth century, the increase in quality British-made point blanket sales

(Above) The earliest of the known labels, the Trademark Type A was used from around 1890 to 1900 and did not include the phrase "The Seal of Quality" found on all later labels.

(Top) Around 1930, Hudson's Bay Company used the simplified Scroll label for a brief period. It was issued in both red and the very rare gold embroidered variants. The gold variant was used for pastel-coloured point blankets.

through outlets other than Hudson's Bay Company caused Hbc management to become concerned that they would lose their preeminent position in the point blanket trade. Probably as early as 1890, but certainly by 1900, Hbc started affixing cloth labels to its blankets at the time of manufacture identifying these wares as "genuine point blankets." This practice led to a prolonged trade battle with one of their former principal suppliers, the Early Company. Because of the number of suits and counter-suits threatened by the two companies, Hbc kept adjusting their labels in an attempt to assert their claim to a virtual monopoly on point blanket sales in Canada. These variations in label design form a series of dating clues that can assist the collector in assigning a date of manufacture to a specific twentieth century Hudson's Bay blanket.

While Hbc used over two dozen variant labels during the last century, they can be classed into four general periods. From about 1890 to just after 1925, when Hudson's Bay Company received its first Trademark Registration for its seal, the company used the "Trademark" and the "Seal" series of labels, which are characterized by a legend around the company's seal.

The second period, from the late 1920s to approximately 1940, includes the use of the smaller-sized "Scroll" and the "Bar" designs, which are simplified in style, mostly with red embroidery (although some gold embroidered examples have been found) and the larger "Stacked" label, which was the first to list the trademark registration numbers for both Canada and the United States. The period from the 1940s to around 1970 includes the rare "All Wool" and the very common "100% Wool" and "100% Wool Dotted" series of labels, which all are gold embroidered on a mid-sized label and predominantly declare the blanket's wool composition. And the final and current period from around 1970 to the turn of the Millennium include the "Bilingual" and "Big Bilingual" labels, which, as their names reflect, incorporate both French and English information in line with late twentieth century Canadian marketing standards.

(Top) From the late 1940s to the 1960s, Hbc issued blankets bearing the 100% Wool label. The 100% Wool Type I label shown here is probably the most common label found on older blankets, indicating the very high volume of sales of point blankets during the early 1950s.

(Left) For the last 25 years, Hbc has used the Big Bilingual label on its point blankets. The Type C variant shown here was introduced in May 2002.

## ON TO THE OLYMPICS

**T**he Hudson's Bay blanket coat was the garment of choice for the Winter Olympic Games for the Canadian athletes and officials in 1936 in Garmisch-Partenkirchen, Germany; in 1960 in Squaw Valley, U.S.A.; in 1964 in Innsbruck, Austria; and in 1968 in Grenoble, France. (Above) Canadian athletes sport the Hbc coat at the opening ceremonies of the winter games in Squaw Valley, 1960, and (right) Canada's Barbara Wagner and Robert Paul (centre) receive their gold medals in figure skating at those games.

## A COAT FOR NORTHERN BEAUTY QUEENS

It was not unusual to see Canadian beauty contestants sporting the famous Hbc garment. In this archival photograph (above) from the late 1920s, the contestants in the Winter Festival Queen Competition in The Pas, Manitoba, pose in their Hbc coats. (Right) In 1966, Miss Muk-Luk waves to the crowd at Polar Park in Edmonton, Alberta.

HUDSON'S BAY *Point* BLANKETS

# A BLANKET MADE TO LAST

To keep a fine point blanket in the best condition a little care is needed. These English-made point blankets are sturdy textiles capable of taking extremely rough handling. After all, they were designed to be hard-used in wilderness life. But to be kept in perfect condition, the blanket should be occasionally brushed clean so that grit and foreign particles cannot be caught in the weave and allowed to break the blanket's structural fibres.

When stored, like all woollen products, care should be taken to avoid the chance of moths colonizing the blanket. Newer point blankets are marketed in plastic or vinyl zippered bags. In a damp climate, these bags should be opened at least once a year, the blanket removed, aired, and refolded to allow fresh air in and excessive humidity to be released so as to avoid the possibility of mildewing.

The best storage, short of a quality cedar chest, is to use blanket bags, preferably made of cotton, which are capable of "breathing" and help avoid the possibility of damage due to excessive humidity. Old cotton pillowcases, found in thrift stores, can be adapted to make excellent storage bags. Blankets left folded should be opened and refolded annually with the pattern of the folds alternated so that permanent creases do not settle in the blanket.

(Opposite) "The world's most famous blankets" proclaimed this 1955 ad. (Right) Blankets left folded should be opened and refolded annually to prevent permanent creases.

71

A quality wool point blanket kept in good condition will rarely need cleaning as often as other textiles. The oils in the wool and the nap itself tend to shed dirt and, thus, occasional brushing should keep the blanket in prime condition. However, in time it may be necessary to

A quality cedar chest is the best place to store a point blanket.

properly clean the blanket. The older, traditionally coloured blankets can be hand-washed, but like all woollen goods only in cool water and with a mild soap, like Woolite™, and then fully rinsed. A washed blanket should never be wrung out; the water must be gently pressed out and the blanket should only be air dried, preferably by spreading the blanket flat on the lawn in the shade rather than being hung to dry. Today, Hudson's Bay Company recommends that the Pastels and all modern blankets be dry cleaned only.

Damage to the weave of the blanket itself, whether from moths or accidents, can be repaired. It is possible to have this done by professional "invisible weaving," a service available at most drycleaners. However, this is usually fairly expensive, and such repairs can be done at home. The main purpose is to limit the damage so that any holes or tears do not have an opportunity to expand. To match the colour of the original blanket or its headings, wool embroidery thread is available in a tremendous variety of colours. The blanket should be taken to a crafts shop and the embroidery thread matched to the blanket in good light, preferably daylight. Small round holes can be lightly darned, but larger holes may require working the thread into the blanket simulating the original weave. A clean cut should be stitched together with the lightest weight embroidery thread available in the matching colour. Often it is possible to unwind the multiple plies of the thread and work with only one fine strand.

With a little care, a fine Hudson's Bay Company point blanket can give a lifetime of service and comfort. To possess one of these finest of blankets is to share a part of the rich heritage of Canada's past.

## "CANADA'S MERCHANTS SINCE 1670"

**H**udson's Bay Company opened its first department store in Winnipeg in 1881 and early in the twentieth century built up the largest retailing enterprise in Canada. Right across the country, "the Bay" stores (as they were known after 1965) opened on downtown main streets and in new suburban shopping centres. Starting with Morgans of Montreal in 1960 and continuing into this century, Hbc absorbed or acquired several distinguished Canadian retailers, including Woodward's, Freiman's, Simpson's, and Zellers.

Today, the world's oldest chartered company reminds people of its rich history with the use of the famous blanket multistripe colours; for example, in a company Christmas card (left) and in the new signage of the Toronto Yorkdale store (below).

## A TESTIMONY TO "OLD FAITHFUL"

**A**round 1930, the Company placed classified advertisements in a number of newspapers in the Pacific Northwest. They asked readers who had Hudson's Bay blankets that were over twenty years old to contact them. They received a large number of letters, but perhaps the best was one from a correspondent in British Columbia:

*Vancouver, B.C., June 26, 1931*

*I have in my possession, one of a pair of blankets which I purchased in your store 30 years ago this month. Used as a saddle blanket during several seasons of riding the range. Was packed through to Revelstoke — thence south through the Kootenays on prospecting and hunting trips. Packed north all through the mountains and received some of the roughest usage that any fabric could possibly survive.*

*I could not truthfully estimate how many tons of river gravel was dumped onto it and washed in our attempts to find gold. Was packed back to Alberta and used on freighting trips to Athabasca Landing and Peace River — also the famous Barr Colony (Lloydminster).*

*Used as a saddle blanket for almost two years of riding around on hard and tough trips for the C.N.R. engineers. Then used for camping during construction of C.N.R. from Battleford to Edmonton, thence to the mountains.*

*Six or seven Indian babies have been born on it — was used during a trip after wild horses in Northern Alberta when one end got burned in a bad prairie fire, leaving about three-quarters of the blanket intact. Used for three years during my homesteading stint.*

*When I got married, I took my young wife on to the homestead, used the blanket as her covering during the eleven-mile drive. Used it on our bed for years. When the youngster arrived, was used as a mattress in bottom of the buggy. When the next one came, was used as a cover on its crib. That winter, was used as part protection*

over a valuable small stock of potatoes. Next winter used as a drop curtain hung in front of a few pure bred poultry. Then thoroughly washed and placed on the bed.

We were out hunting in a car, got stuck in mud and placed the blanket under the back wheel; the wheel spun, then gripped and out we came, leaving a hole in one corner of Old Faithful. Part of it I cut off and sewed up into a pair of heavy socks and used them all winter during a mail trip.

We still have the old blanket after thirty years of service, somewhat faded certainly, but like Johnny Walker, still going strong. During all those years the only hole is where the auto wheel ground it. It never frayed, and only during the last few years of very rough usage did it fade.

(Above) Two Canadian icons — the canoe and the Hbc point blanket — on display at the Canadian Canoe Museum in Peterborough, Ontario.

# EPILOGUE

Today the distinctive multistripe design of the Hudson's Bay Company's best-known point blanket is recognizable in the Bay's advertising, store credit card motifs, shopping bags, and department store signage. Over the past 75 years, the vast amount of correspondence that Hudson's Bay Company has received concerning point blankets reflects the fascination of owners and collectors with the lore of a blanket that has "covered centuries." The Hudson's Bay point blanket has proven its durability and quality in both camp and home for over 200 years, firmly establishing it as part of the history and fabric of Canadian life.

# INDEX

# PICTURE CREDITS

Every effort has been made to correctly attribute all material reproduced in this book. If any errors have unwittingly occurred, we will be happy to correct them in future editions.

HBCA: Hudson's Bay Company Archives, Provincial Archives of Manitoba
NA/NAC: National Archives of Canada

Front cover and page 1: HBCA, *The Beaver,* Winter 1956
Back cover: HBCA, *The Beaver,* June 1950
**3** Kevin Fleming
**4–5** With permission of the Royal Ontario Museum © ROM, 949.39.20
**6** Hbc Corporate Collection
**7** Harold Tichenor
**8** (left) HBCA 1987/363-B-20; (right) NAC C-17338; (bottom) NAC C-99255
**9** (top and middle) Kevin Fleming; (bottom) Hbc Corporate Collection
**10** Kevin Fleming
**11** Hbc Corporate Collection
**12** HBCA RB FC 3212 CF facing p. 211 (N7602)
**13** HBCA 1987/363-T-32/27 (N3912)
**14** Hbc Corporate Collection
**15** Kevin Fleming
**16–17** HBCA P-181 (T14516)
**18** HBCA 1987/363-W-114/1 (N15182)

**19** HBCA 1987/363-W-114/3 (N14311)
**20** Art Gallery of Hamilton, gift of Mrs. C.H. Stern, 1957
**21** Courtesy of West Oxfordshire Tourism
**22** Private Collection/ Bridgeman Art Library
**25** Rochdale Art Gallery, Lancashire, UK/Bridgeman Art Library
**26** © Adam Woolfitt/CORBIS
**27** Hulton-Deutsch Collection/CORBIS
**28** (top and bottom) Hulton-Deutsch Collection/CORBIS
**30–31** Hbc Corporate Collection
**33** HBCA *Moccasin Telegraph,* Summer 1979, pp. 60–61
**35** HBCA P-180
**36–37** HBCA, *The Beaver,* December 1930
**38** HBCA 1987/363-W-114/5 (N7165)
**39** HBCA, *The Beaver,* May 1922
**40** (top) no known source; (bottom) HBCA P-116 (T5508)
**41** © 1943 Elizabeth Burris-Meyer and Eleanor Beckham. *This is Fashion.* Harper & Brothers Publishers.
**42–43** Provincial Archives of Alberta, neg. no. 177. Courtesy of A. Smith Bagan.
**44** HBCA 1987/363-W-114/9

**45** (top) Provincial Archives of Alberta, neg. no. B.992. Courtesy of A. Smith Bagan; (bottom) Courtesy of A. Smith Bagan
**46** (left) © Francis Back 1988; (right) NA-667-182. Glenbow Archives: Arnold Lupson. Courtesy of A. Smith Bagan
**47** NAC-C7376, C. Horetsky. Courtesy of A. Smith Bagan
**48** HBCA 1987/363-W-114/2 (N15183)
**49** HBCA, *The Beaver,* Winter 1956
**50–51** HBCA, *The Beaver,* November 1921
**52** (inset) HBCA, *The Beaver,* December 1926; HBCA 1987/363-W-116/104 (N15188)
**53** HBCA, *The Beaver,* December 1939 (N15179)
**54–55** HBCA 1987/363-W-115/50
**56** HBCA, *The Beaver,* December 1929; (inset) HBCA, *The Beaver,* December 1930
**57** (top) HBCA 1987/363-W-115/57 © Brander Studios, Edmonton; (bottom) HBCA, *The Beaver,* 1953
**58** HBC blanket brochure, no date
**59** (left) HBCA Vertical File, *The Beaver,* 2000/24, Blankets; HBC blanket brochure, no date

**60** (top) HBCA, *The Beaver,* October 1922; (left) HBC, no date; (right) HBCA 1987/363-W-117/52 (N15178)
**61** HBC blanket brochure, no date
**62** (top and bottom) HBCA, Verticle File, *The Beaver,* 2000/24, Blankets
**64** (top) HBCA 1987/363-M-67/8 (N7458); (middle) HBCA 1987/363-M-67/6 (N7456); (bottom) HBCA 1987/363-M-67/9 (N7459)/Laurel Co Inc.
**65** (left) HBCA 1987/363-M-67/5 (N15181); (right top) NBCA 1987/363-C-210/31 (N15180); (right bottom) HBCA 1987/363-W-316/64 (N15192)
**66–67** Courtesy of Harold Tichenor
**68** (top) HBCA 1987/363-W-118/30 © Canada Wide Photo; (bottom) COA
**69** (top) HBCA; (bottom) HBCA 1987/363-W-117/67 © Ranson
**70** HBCA, *The Beaver,* Autumn 1955
**71** Hbc Corporate Collection
**72** Hbc Corporate Collection
**73** (top and bottom) Hbc Corporate Collection
**74–75** Canadian Canoe Museum
**76–77** Hbc Corporate Collection

# BIBLIOGRAPHY

Back, Francis. 1990. "The Trade Blanket in New France." *The Museum of the Fur Trade Quarterly* 26, no. 3: 2–8.

Gaede, Frederick C. and E. Bryce Workman. 1979. "Notes on Point Blankets in the Military Service." *The Museum of the Fur Trade Quarterly* 15, no. 2: 1–4.

Hudson's Bay Company Archive A. 6/20.

Johnson, A. M. 1956. "Mons. Maugenest Suggests…." *The Beaver* (summer): 49–53.

Kapoun, Robert W. and Charles J. Lohrmann. 1992. *Language of the Robe.* Layton, Utah: Gibbs Smith.

Krause, Aurel. 1979. *The Tlingit Indians.* Translated by Erna Gunter. Vancouver: Douglas and McIntyre. (Originally published in German in 1885.)

Miller, Jay. 2000. "Alaskan Tlingit and Tsimshian." American Indians of the Pacific Northwest Digital Collection. University of Washington. Retrieved June 24, 2002, from http://content.lib.washington.edu/aipnw/miller1/tsimshian.html.

Tichenor, Harold. 2002. *A Collector's Guide to Point Blankets of the Hudson's Bay Company and Other Companies Trading in North America.* Bowen Island, B.C.: Cinetel Film Productions Ltd.

# ACKNOWLEDGEMENTS

**Q**uantum Books would like to thank Brenda Hobbs and Joan Murray of Hbc Heritage and Debra Moore of the Hudson's Bay Company Archives for their invaluable help during the course of this project. And many thanks to Anne Smith Bagan, author of "Blanket Coats of the Blackfoot First Nations" (unpublished Masters Thesis, University of Alberta, 1997), for contributing the feature on The Capote, which appears on page 46.

*About the author:* Harold Tichenor is an accomplished documentary and dramatic film producer whose credits include the Emmy-nominated miniseries "Children of the Dust." He has previously published articles on film history and stereo photography. Harold currently lives on Bowen Island, British Columbia and in West Kootenai, Montana, where he houses his extensive collection of Hbc blankets and photographic art.

*Editorial Director:*
Hugh Brewster

*Associate Editorial Director:*
Wanda Nowakowska

*Art Director:*
Gordon Sibley

*Consulting Editor:*
Ian R. Coutts

*Project Editor:*
Catherine Fraccaro

*Editorial Assistance:*
Laurie Coulter, Imoinda Romain

*Graphic Production:*
Nathan Beyerle

*Production Director:*
Susan Barrable

*Production Manager:*
Sandra L. Hall

*Colour Separation:*
Colour Technologies

*Printing and Binding:*
Friesens Corporation

THE BLANKET: AN ILLUSTRATED HISTORY OF THE HUDSON'S BAY POINT BLANKET was produced by Madison Press Books, which is under the direction of Albert E. Cummings

*For over 330 years, Hudson's Bay Company has had a single mission: to be responsive to the needs and wants of Canadian customers, offering value, quality, and service, backed by a name they trust. While the mission hasn't changed, Canadian customers and society have. In 1670, a single store could fulfill the mission. Today's customers need more choice and convenience and they can find it through the Hbc family of stores — the Bay, Zellers, Home Outfitters, and Hbc.com. As Canada's largest department store retailer, Hudson's Bay Company has over 500 locations from coast to coast.*

Text, design, and compilation
© 2002 Hudson's Bay Company

**National Library of Canada Cataloguing in Publication Data**

Tichenor, Harold
   The blanket : an illustrated history of the Hudson's Bay point blanket / Harold Tichenor.

"A Quantum book produced for Hudson's Bay Company."
Includes bibliographical references and index.

ISBN 1-895892-20-1

1. Hudson's Bay blankets— History. 1. Hudson's Bay Company II. Title.

TT405.T53 2002          677'.626
C2002-903537-6

Produced by
Madison Press Books for the Quantum Book Group Inc.
1000 Yonge Street, Suite 200
Toronto, Ontario M4W 2K2

*Printed in Canada*

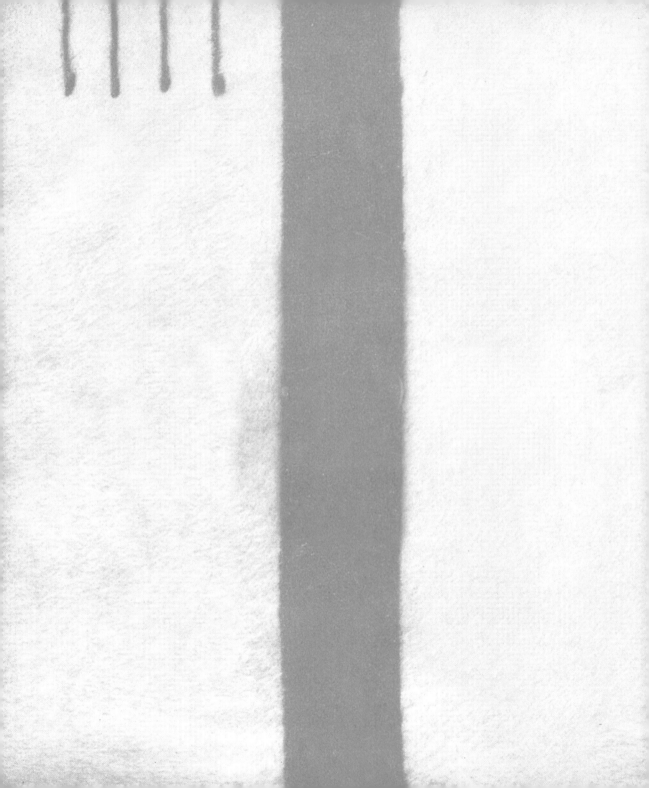